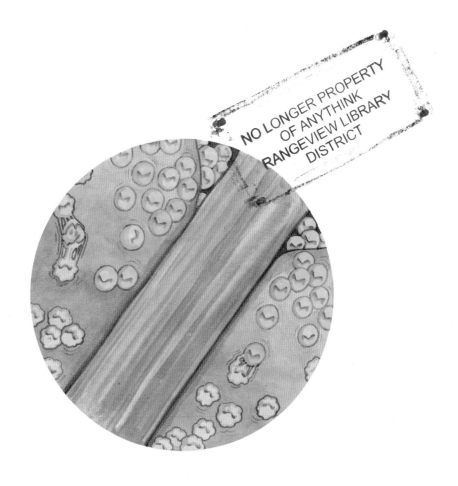

D0731396

Antibiotics Timeline

ca. 3300 BCE

Prehistoric warriors in northern Europe pack their wounds with moss to stop the bleeding and prevent infection.

ca. 500 CE

In Central America, the Mayans put maggots into wounds to eat away rotting flesh.

1847

Ignaz Semmelweis insists that doctors wash their hands between cutting up dead bodies and dealing with patients.

ca. 3000 BCE

Ancient Egyptians use honey and fat on open wounds to keep out germs.

1536

Ambroise Paré uses a mixture of egg yolk, turpentine, and oil of roses to treat injured soldiers.

1865

Joseph Lister sprays carbolic acid in the operating room—germs don't stand a chance.

1950

Antibiotics are in widespread use, saving millions of lives.

21st Century

Hospitals struggle against antibiotic-resistant bacteria. Good hygiene is still the best defense against infection.

1862

Louis Pasteur discovers that bacteria are spoiling his broth.

1928

Alexander Fleming finds that the mold penicillium kills bacteria.

Know Your Enemy

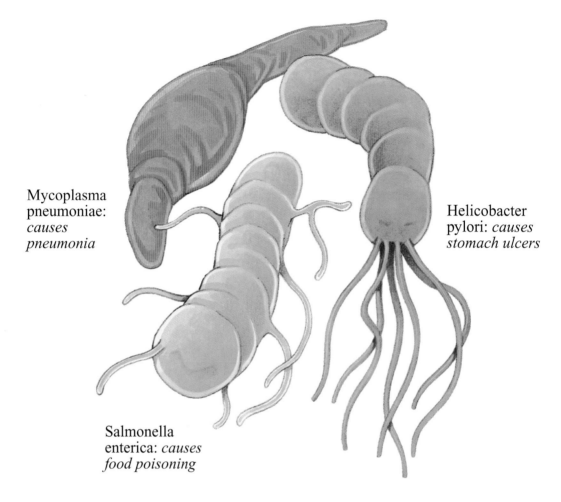

Mycoplasma pneumoniae: *causes pneumonia*

Salmonella enterica: *causes food poisoning*

Helicobacter pylori: *causes stomach ulcers*

Bacteria come in many different shapes, but not many sizes. Almost all are so small, they can be seen only with a microscope. Though there are lots of bacteria that don't cause illnesses, those that do each cause only certain diseases. It's vital to find the right antibiotic to kill the infection. An antibiotic that cures pneumonia (a serious lung condition) won't necessarily help fight against the bacteria that cause stomach ulcers (breaks in the lining of the stomach).

Author:

Anne Rooney studied English at Cambridge University, England, and then earned a Ph.D. at Cambridge. She has held teaching posts at several UK universities and is currently a Royal Literary Fund fellow at Newnham College, Cambridge. She has written more than 150 books for children and adults, including several on the history of science and medicine. She also writes children's fiction.

Artist:

David Antram was born in Brighton, England, in 1958. He studied at Eastbourne College of Art and then worked in advertising for 15 years before becoming a full-time artist. He has illustrated many children's nonfiction books.

Series creator:

David Salariya was born in Dundee, Scotland. He has illustrated a wide range of books and has created and designed many new series for publishers in the UK and overseas. David established The Salariya Book Company in 1989. He lives in Brighton with his wife, illustrator Shirley Willis, and their son, Jonathan.

Editors: **Stephen Haynes, Caroline Coleman**

Editorial Assistant: **Mark Williams**

PAPER FROM SUSTAINABLE FORESTS

Published in Great Britain in 2015 by
The Salariya Book Company Ltd
25 Marlborough Place, Brighton BN1 1UB

ISBN-13: 978-0-531-21218-9 (lib. bdg.) 978-0-531-21309-4 (pbk.)

All rights reserved.
Published in 2015 in the United States
by Franklin Watts
An imprint of Scholastic Inc.
Published simultaneously in Canada.

A CIP catalog record for this book is available
from the Library of Congress.

Printed and bound in China.
Printed on paper from sustainable sources.

1 2 3 4 5 6 7 8 9 10 R 24 23 22 21 20 19 18 17 16 15

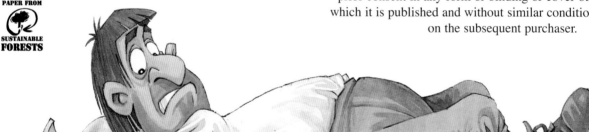

You Wouldn't Want to Live Without™

Antibiotics!

Written by
Anne Rooney

Illustrated by
David Antram

Created and designed by
David Salariya

Franklin Watts®
An Imprint of Scholastic Inc.
NEW YORK • TORONTO • LONDON • AUCKLAND • SYDNEY
MEXICO CITY • NEW DELHI • HONG KONG
DANBURY, CONNECTICUT

Contents

Introduction

You wouldn't have wanted to have a nasty injury or infection a hundred years ago. Of course, you don't want one now, either, but at least now there are medicines, called antibiotics, to help you get better. If you get appendicitis, a badly broken leg, or even a deep cut, you aren't likely to die—but that hasn't always been true. When you have an injury, microbes from the air and the environment swarm in. Many of these are bacteria that love living in wounds. Lots of illnesses are caused by bacteria that you breathe in or swallow, too. Even though they're extremely tiny, bacteria multiply over and over until they can overwhelm your body and make you very sick, or even kill you. Antibiotics kill bacteria. So, as you read on, think: How would you like to live without antibiotics?

A plague doctor in the 17th century. The mask was thought to protect the doctor from "bad air." But we know now that plague is caused by the bacteria shown on page 23.

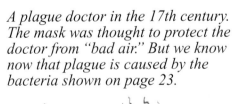

Safety Warning

Some of the tips in this book may be useful if you ever get transported back in time. But if you're hurt or sick now, go to the doctor!

I'm going to die of fright, doctor!

Your Body Is a Battlefield

Usually, your skin keeps nasty bugs and germs out of your body. But if your skin is cut, germs can rush in. Once inside the nice, wet, warm environment of your body, they settle down to do what they do best—reproduce!

Your body's immune system does its best to fight off germs, but it can't always manage alone. That's when antibiotics come in handy. They help your body in the battle against bacteria.

But don't think you're safe just because you don't have a nasty cut. Germs are all around you, including in the air, in the soil, on things you touch, and even in your food. Bacteria you swallow or breathe in can make you sick. If your immune system isn't strong enough, antibiotics can come to your rescue again. They work like reinforcements, giving your body extra troops to fight bacteria.

Aaargh!

AN ARROW through the leg makes a nasty wound. And a dirty arrow on a muddy battlefield will carry millions of bacteria straight into the hole. This is going to get messy!

Splinter

EVEN A SPLINTER of that arrow carries thousands of bacteria, ready to settle in and multiply.

Bacteria

Phagocytes

WHITE BLOOD CELLS, or phagoctyes, rush to attack the intruders.

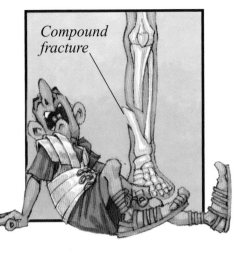
Compound fracture

BREAK A LEG! If a broken bone sticks through the skin, it's called a compound fracture. It used to be a death sentence. Very few people survived compound fractures, because of infection.

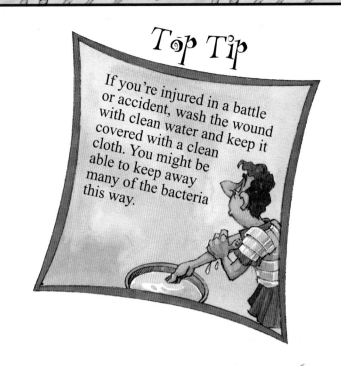
Top Tip

If you're injured in a battle or accident, wash the wound with clean water and keep it covered with a clean cloth. You might be able to keep away many of the bacteria this way.

IT'S LOOKING BAD as the wound oozes pus (below) and feels hot and sore. The phagocytes can't eat the bacteria fast enough.

Stiff upper lip, man!

IN ANCIENT TIMES, there's only one way to get rid of the bacteria in the leg —that's to get rid of the leg. This is going to hurt.

Microbes

MICROBES have been around for a very long time—more than 3 billion years! There are four main types, but most illnesses are caused by two types: bacteria and viruses. Not all of them are out to get you, though: many kinds help you to run your body, and you couldn't live without them. But some make you sick.

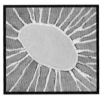
Bacterium

Fungus

Protist

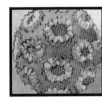
Virus

BACTERIUM VS. VIRUS
Most microbes that cause illness are either bacteria or viruses. Bacteria are bigger and are alive. Viruses are just strands of genetic material surrounded by protein.

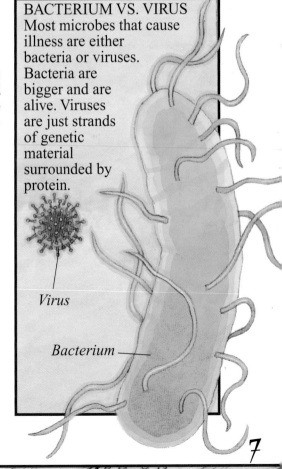
Virus

Bacterium

Which Would You Choose: Maggots or Moss?

L ying injured on a battlefield for so long that flies lay eggs in your wounds and maggots hatch and start to eat you doesn't sound great. But it could save your life!

It used to be common to welcome maggots into a festering wound. Soldiers and doctors on battlefields popped in a few maggots to chomp away on rotting and infected flesh. The Aborigines of Australia did it. The Maya of Central America did it. Even prisoners in World War II prison camps did it.

No maggots around? Try moss. It's springy and absorbent—great for soaking up blood. It also has natural antibiotic properties that help prevent infection, though no one knew that until recently.

MAGGOTS eat the infected flesh first. But if you leave them in the wound too long they eat the healthy parts, too, and make things worse.

Time's up with my maggots!

Moss

Maggots

8

AN ANCIENT HUNTER was found frozen in ice on a mountain in Italy in 1991—5,300 years after he died. Archaeologists named him Ötzi. He had packed moss into a deep wound on his hand, which kept his hand from getting infected.

Top Tip

If you're injured on a battlefield with no first aid kit, put moss over your wounds, but make sure it's clean. Pick out the dirt first—there are lots of bacteria in soil. If you can find a maggot, too, all the better!

BLOODSUCKING LEECH, anyone? These worms have a chemical in their saliva that keeps blood from clotting, so they can keep sucking. Doctors used them for centuries to prevent bruising and break up blood clots.

KEEPING A WOUND CLOSED with stitches helps to keep bacteria out and prevent infection. No needle or thread? Try East African soldier ants.

HOLD THE EDGES of the wound together and trick the ant into biting through them.

NOW SNAP OFF the body, leaving the head and pincers in place. There you are: stitches, even in the remote jungle!

Don't Worry About the Mold— It's Good For You!

Have you ever seen food that's gone moldy? You probably threw it away. Mold is a microbe—a type of fungus. Lots of molds produce antibiotics. Many of our antibiotic medicines are made from different types of fungus. This means that sometimes eating something "bad" can be good for people. (But not always—don't go around eating moldy foods!)

SOME MOLDS are added to food on purpose. Cheeses with a furry skin, like Brie, have mold on the outside. Blue cheeses have mold on the inside, in the veins. These molds are safe to eat.

IN THE PAST, poor people often had to make do with moldy food. Perhaps it kept them from getting some of the infections that wealthier people got.

Rich and sick

A FOLK REMEDY for boils and wounds was a poultice of bread and milk. Pour milk on the bread to make a mush and slap it on. Handy if you get a little hungry, too.

SALIVA has chemicals in it that help fight bacteria. That's why animals lick their wounds—and perhaps how we got the idea that a kiss can "make it better"!

You Can Do It!

Grow your own mold! Take a piece of bread, put it in a plastic bag, and leave it somewhere fairly warm. Then wait. Soon, mold will grow on the bread. But don't eat it! Breathing in mold can be bad for you, so throw it away without opening the bag.

Hot or Cold?

Sizzle

AN OLD WAY of treating wounds was to burn them with a red-hot iron or boiling oil. Many patients died of shock or from infections.

IN 1536, French army surgeon Ambroise Paré ran out of boiling oil. He tried using egg yolks, turpentine, and oil of roses instead.

RESULT! Paré's mixture kept air from the wound and stopped bacteria from growing. It was a lot less painful—and his patients got better.

Poor but well

Do You Want Sugar With That Wound?

Honey and sugar are nice when you're hurt—and not just to eat. People have used honey or sugar on wounds for thousands of years, even without understanding how they work. A layer of honey poured over the open surface of a wound seals it so that the air can't get to it. Without air, bacteria can't grow and so the wound doesn't become infected.

But the honey has other important effects, too. Some types of honey change the level of acidity of the wound, making it hostile to bacteria.

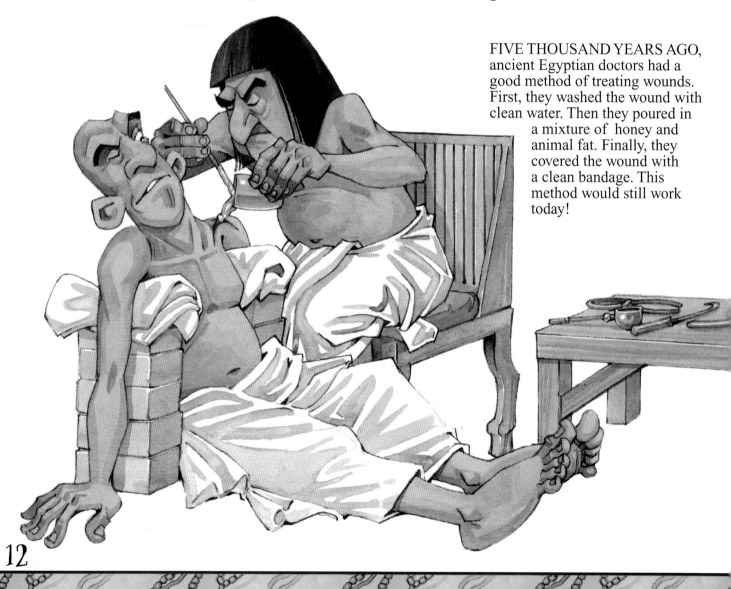

FIVE THOUSAND YEARS AGO, ancient Egyptian doctors had a good method of treating wounds. First, they washed the wound with clean water. Then they poured in a mixture of honey and animal fat. Finally, they covered the wound with a clean bandage. This method would still work today!

Honey's sugariness draws a body fluid called lymph to the area, which helps to remove dead tissue.

Honey also has natural antibiotic properties that help to kill off bacteria in the wound. Doctors are looking again at honey and finding out how it works to help wounds heal.

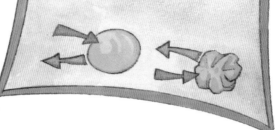

How It Works

Water moves through cell walls toward an area with a higher concentration of salt or sugar. This means that putting sugar on a wound draws water out of the bacteria, making them shrivel up and die.

HONEY is a syrup made by bees from the nectar that they collect from flowers. The bees add a chemical to honey when they make it, called defensin-1, which works as an antibiotic.

PACKING SUGAR into a wound can help to prevent infection. This works even with the internal wounds made by surgery.

It's not for you. It's for the bacteria.

13

Now Wash Your Hands

Before anesthetics were available to keep people from feeling pain, surgery hurt—a lot. Surgeons could carry out only very quick and simple operations, such as sawing off legs and digging out bullets. Operations on internal organs weren't possible—they would be too painful and the patient would move around too much.

With anesthetics, developed in the 1840s, surgeons could do more. But opening up the body let in bacteria, and many patients died of infections. At the time, doctors didn't know about bacteria or that they caused infections. That's why they didn't know not to operate with dirty hands.

That all changed in 1865 when British surgeon Joseph Lister discovered that if he operated in a spray of carbolic acid, his patients rarely died. He had discovered antisepsis: making the area of the wound unsuitable for bacteria to live, so they don't even get a foothold.

Birth and Death

IN 1847, Ignaz Semmelweis worked in a hospital in Vienna, Austria. Women in one maternity ward died much more often than women in another ward. He investigated and found that doctors were coming to deliver babies right after cutting up dead bodies.

LISTER'S FIRST operation using carbolic acid as a disinfectant was on a boy with a compound fracture. Without Lister's help, the boy certainly would have died, since compound fractures always became infected.

Such a fuss!

THE DOCTORS didn't like being told to wash their hands, but the deaths stopped because of Semmelweis's discovery.

SEMMELWEIS suspected the doctors were contaminating the women by coming straight from handling dead bodies to the maternity ward. To test his theory, he insisted the doctors wash their hands and change their clothes after cutting up bodies.

You Can Do It!

You can do your part to stop infections by washing your hands before you eat, after you use the toilet, and after sneezing or coughing—as well as when you get dirty! Simple hand-washing with soap is a great way to avoid getting sick.

Keep spraying, please. I like mist.

Can You Spot the Enemy?

In the 1860s, French scientist Louis Pasteur figured out that microbes were responsible for a disease that was killing silkworms. He soon found that microbes also cause milk and wine to go bad, and that microbes cause many human diseases as well. Some of the microbes he studied were bacteria.

Pasteur showed that microbes are carried in the air. Before that, people thought they just appeared out of nowhere. That would make them a lot harder to fight!

PASTEUR boiled broth in a flask with a long, curved neck so that dust carrying microbes couldn't get inside. His broth didn't go bad.

FOR CENTURIES people believed that living things could spring up from matter. They thought maggots just appeared from rotting meat and that fleas were produced by dust.

PASTEUR could find microbes for some diseases—he could see them with his microscope. But others were too small to find.

THE MICROBES Pasteur couldn't see were viruses. We can see them with an electron microscope, but that wasn't invented until long after Pasteur died.

SICK SILKWORMS led Pasteur to discover that bacteria cause disease. He was investigating because the French silk industry was losing money when the silkworms died.

Top Tip

To keep food from going bad, cover it while it's very hot. After it has cooled, put it in the refrigerator. Bacteria can't grow as quickly at lower temperatures. If you heat food up, make sure it's really hot, because heat can kill bacteria that may have grown in it.

Let's see what we can see...

Are We There Yet?

How would you like some soup made with dirty bandages? No? That's what two German doctors, Rudolph Emmerich and Oskar Löw (sometimes spelled Loew), made in the 1890s. They took used bandages and extracted a bacterium that occurs in open wounds. They discovered that their bacteria "soup" could kill the bacteria that cause the deadly diseases diphtheria, cholera, typhoid, and anthrax. They'd made the first antibiotic: pyocyanase. There were other early trials, too.

EMMERICH AND LÖW made the first antibiotic used in hospitals, but it didn't work equally well on all people. Unfortunately, it was also rather poisonous. Some patients got better, but others got worse or even died. Pyocyanase was soon abandoned.

IN 1885, Victor Babeș discovered that some microbes produce chemicals that kill other microbes. It was a key discovery—it explains how antibiotics work.

ARNALDO CANTANI noticed that when patients died of tuberculosis (TB), the bacteria that caused the disease disappeared from the patients' lungs soon afterward. He guessed that the same bacteria that made dead bodies rot also killed the TB bacteria. So he made a broth from these bacteria, and asked a patient with TB to breathe in the fumes. She got better.

Take one now, and one if you wake up in the morning.

Top Tip

Don't reuse a bandage you've placed on a wound. Bacteria from one wound can infect another if you use a dirty dressing. And certainly never make soup out of your old bandages!

SULFA CRAZE. The first really successful antibiotics were sulfa drugs, discovered in 1932. They saved thousands of lives during World War II, but they weren't properly tested, and lots of people died from taking them.

MAGIC BULLET. Paul Ehrlich set out to find a "magic bullet"—a chemical drug that would kill the microbes that cause a disease, without harming the human body. He found an arsenic compound, called arsphenamine. Beginning in 1912, it was sold as Salvarsan.

19

Fleming and His Moldy Plates

Scientists grow bacteria on dishes of special jelly. You wouldn't want to eat it, but microbes like it!

Do you always clean up your room? Luckily, Alexander Fleming didn't. His messy habits led him to discover the mold penicillium, from which we now make the important antibiotic penicillin.

When Fleming went on vacation

in 1928, he left dishes of agar (a special type of jelly) piled up in his laboratory. He had been growing bacteria on them. When he got back, he noticed clear spaces where the bacteria had been killed off by something. That something was penicillium, which had landed on his plates and begun to grow.

Fleming didn't make penicillin from his discovery, however. He left that task to others.

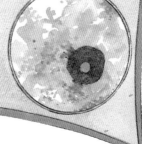

The penicillium mold produces a chemical that leaks out onto the agar plate. The chemical is poisonous to bacteria—it's an antibiotic—so they die, leaving a clear space on the plate.

HOWARD FLOREY (left) was the first to make a penicillin medicine and try it out on a patient. The man improved a little, but then he died. Florey hadn't made enough of the medicine.

ERNST CHAIN worked with Howard Florey to make a usable medicine from penicillin. Together, they investigated exactly how it worked and looked at other possible sources of antibiotics. They decided penicillium was the best.

PRETTY PLATES. Fleming used to amuse himself and his friends by making art with microbes. He injected colored bacteria onto agar plates in patterns. When the bacteria grew, the picture appeared.

21

What's Going On?

A bacterium is a living organism, even though it has only one cell. It takes in nutrients and grows, just like other organisms, such as cats and dogs.

But unlike cats and dogs, a bacterium reproduces by splitting in two. When you have an infection, the bacteria inside you reproduce constantly. They can double every 20 to 30 minutes! A high temperature, pus, and not feeling well are side effects of your body battling the bacteria.

Antibiotics interfere with how the bacteria work. Some antibiotics stop a process that bacteria need to stay alive, and others prevent them from reproducing.

THIS BACTERIUM is shown many times larger than its real size. It's actually so small that at least 10,000 could line up across your thumbnail. The tail, called a flagellum, allows the bacterium to swim.

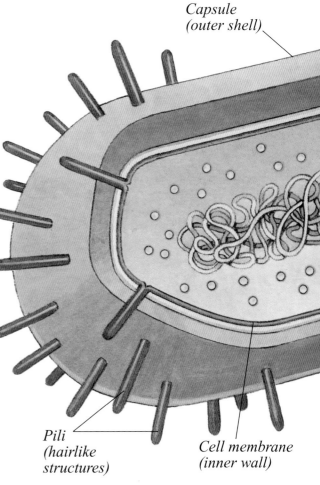

Capsule (outer shell)

Pili (hairlike structures)

Cell membrane (inner wall)

Bacteria Babies!

WHEN A BACTERIUM is ready to reproduce, the part of the cell that holds its genetic information (its DNA) copies itself. The two copies separate, the cell grows larger, and then a dividing wall grows across the middle. When it's all ready, the two cells separate.

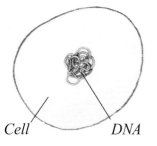

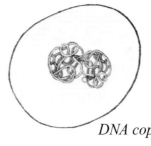

Cell   *DNA*   *DNA copies itself...*

*Cytoplasm
(a gel-like substance)*

*DNA (genetic
material)*

Flagellum (tail)

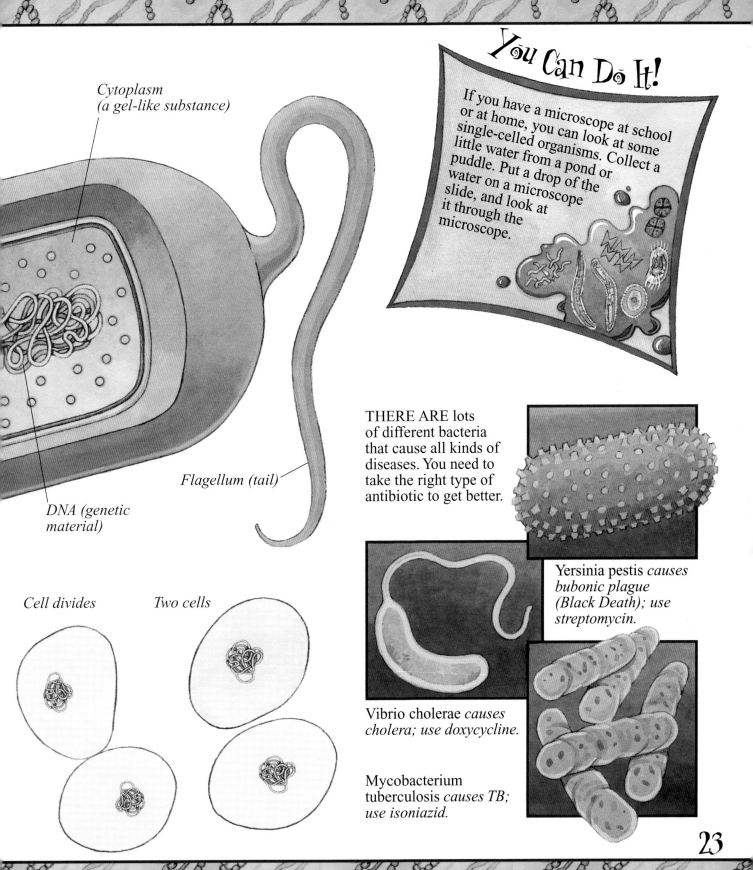

THERE ARE lots of different bacteria that cause all kinds of diseases. You need to take the right type of antibiotic to get better.

Yersinia pestis *causes bubonic plague (Black Death); use streptomycin.*

Cell divides   *Two cells*

Vibrio cholerae *causes cholera; use doxycycline.*

Mycobacterium tuberculosis *causes TB; use isoniazid.*

23

Antibiotics Everywhere

After penicillin was invented, scientists started looking around for more antibiotics. They found them in all kinds of places. Many, like penicillin, come from molds, and lots of those molds live in the soil. Although it's always a good idea to wash dirt out of a wound, some dirt might have antibiotic molds in it. So you wash the dirt out, and then you might treat the wound with—something from dirt!

When a microorganism that makes an antibiotic is found, scientists grow it in huge tanks. It's like a giant, liquid farm for microbes.

TAKING ANTIBIOTICS. If you are sick, you might take antibiotics in liquid form or in a pill, or in serious cases through an intravenous drip. If you have an injury, you might rub on an antibiotic cream.

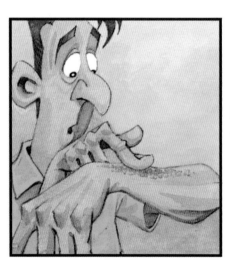

MANY ANTIBIOTICS produce side effects—they make people a bit sick in other ways while helping them to get better. Common side effects include an upset stomach or a rash. Most side effects are minor, but if you experience one, tell your doctor.

THE ANTIBIOTIC NYSTATIN is used to treat fungal infections in people. But it's also used on valuable paintings that have gotten wet and been damaged by mold. Nystatin is also given to sick trees with Dutch elm disease.

Timeline

1877 Louis Pasteur and Jules Joubert discover that one microbe can be used to fight another.

1942 Commercial manufacture of penicillin starts. Penicillin saves lives during World War II.

1943 Discovery of streptomycin made from bacteria that live in soil; it's used to treat TB but can have serious side effects. It can also kill algae in fish tanks.

1952 Erythromycin is found in another bacterium that lives in soil.

You Can Do It!

Make a list of the times when you or someone in your family—including your pets—have had antibiotics in the last few years. What might have happened if you hadn't had them?

1877
1942
1943
1952

1953 Tetracycline is developed. It's effective against many types of bacteria. The Nubians, neighbors of the ancient Egyptians, used it accidentally in their beer.

1972 Amoxicillin is the first semisynthetic antibiotic—a natural antibiotic that has been changed by scientists to make it more useful or to have fewer side effects.

1953

1972

BIG FAT COWS. In the 1940s, scientists discovered by accident that feeding farm animals a small amount of antibiotic made them stay healthier and grow larger.

Too Many, Too Fast

As we've used antibiotics more and more, bacteria have adapted to resist them. Scientists look for new antibiotics all the time, and for ways to improve those we have. But—at least for now—the bacteria are winning.

Some new infections are resistant to most antibiotics, and some old infections have changed so that our medicines no longer work on them. Sometimes we can combat an infection by taking a mixture of different antibiotics together.

WE CAN BLAME those fat cows. Farmers use antibiotics to make their animals grow large quickly, so the farmers can make more money from their meat. Many more antibiotics are used in farming now than in treating sick people.

COWS, CHICKENS, PIGS, and even fish are fed antibiotics by farmers in many parts of the world, including the United States and Asia (but not in the European Union). The low, uneven dose of antibiotics gives bacteria living in those animals the chance to get used to the medicines.

Antibiotics in cattle feed

BACTERIA that have developed resistance to antibiotics multiply inside the animals. They are also passed into the soil and into river water from animal waste.

Cĥomp!

Top Tip

If your doctor doesn't prescribe antibiotics when you're sick, there's probably a good reason. The doctor probably thinks that your body can fight the infection alone, or that you have a viral disease. Antibiotics can't do anything at all to fight viruses.

THE MEAT from these animals brings antibiotic-resistant bacteria into our homes and refrigerators. If meat or fish is not cooked all the way through, or if it touches other food that we eat uncooked, we may accidentally eat live bacteria. These might cause an infection that can't be treated with antibiotics.

Antibiotic-resistant bacteria

ALWAYS FINISH your course of antibiotics. If you don't, any surviving bacteria can develop resistance. Then the antibiotic won't work for you next time you need it.

So, Would You Want to Live Without Antibiotics?

If we can't stop bacteria from evolving to be resistant to antibiotics, we might have to do without antibiotics all over again. Some doctors are taking another look at age-old methods: they're digging out the maggots and honey! Hospitals are working harder to keep very clean to try to prevent infections from starting.

At the same time, scientists are always looking for new, stronger antibiotics to help us fight back against disease. Who knows what will happen—will the bacteria win, or will we find some completely new solution?

DOCTORS TODAY use special, medical-grade maggots to clean wounds. Sometimes they're put inside a thin fabric envelope (below) so they can't escape into the wound.

Nothing is resistant to maggots!

Maggot,
4–7 days

Egg,
8–24 hours

Pupa,
10–20 days

Adult fly

Someone has to come up with the next medical breakthrough so that we can stay on top of the battle against bacteria. If you have what it takes, it could be you! Have you considered a career in medical research?

MEDICAL MAGGOTS are the larvae of flies called blowflies. The flies lay eggs, which hatch into maggots. The maggots turn into pupae. Inside the pupa, the maggot turns into a fly.

ONE WAY TO FIGHT GERMS is to keep hospitals superclean, or "aseptic." Deep cleaning with hot steam and disinfectants kills bacteria that might cause infections.

MRSA (methicillin-resistant *Staphylococcus aureus*) is a germ that can make people very ill. It's resistant to most antibiotics. *Staphylococcus aureus* is the bacterium that led Fleming to penicillin.

SPECIAL MEDICAL-GRADE MAGGOTS are bred in sterile conditions. Ordinary flies visit dog poo and dead rats, but these maggots are superclean and straight from the maggot farm.

Glossary

Absorbent Able to soak up liquids.

Anesthetic A substance that prevents a patient from feeling pain.

Antibiotic A medicine that kills bacteria.

Antisepsis Acting to kill microorganisms that cause infection.

Aseptic Completely lacking in microorganisms that cause infection.

Bacteria (singular: **bacterium**) Single-celled microorganisms. Some types cause disease; others are harmless or even helpful.

Blood clot A lump in the blood inside or outside a blood vessel.

Cell A tiny component of a plant or animal. There are different types, such as muscle cells and blood cells.

Disinfectant A chemical that acts to kill any microorganisms that might cause infection.

Genetic material The complex chemicals DNA and RNA, which carry the information that describes an organism. DNA is somewhat like a recipe for making an organism.

Immune system The body's own defense mechanism to help it fight infection.

Infection Disease or illness caused by the action of a microorganism.

Intravenous drip A tube attached to a blood vessel to deliver medicine slowly, directly into the blood.

Larva The first stage after hatching of an organism (such as an insect) that goes through different stages as it grows. The larva is the form that hatches from the egg.

Lymph A thin fluid that washes through the body, in the lymphatic system. It helps to carry away waste, such as dead cells.

Maternity ward A hospital ward in which women give birth to babies.

Microbe See **microorganism**.

Microorganism An organism that is too small to see without a microscope.

Nectar A sugary syrup produced by flowers to attract insects.

Organism Any living being, such as a plant, animal, or fungus.

Penicillin An antibiotic extracted from the mold penicillium.

Phagocyte A type of white blood cell that attacks hostile cells (such as bacteria) and destroys them.

Poultice A damp pad applied to a wound or injury. It can be made of fabric, cotton, or even bread.

Protist A general term for various simple organisms, often single-celled.

Pupa A stage in the development of an organism in which it changes from a larva to the adult form.

Pus A thick, yellowish substance that sometimes oozes from wounds or boils. It is mostly made up of dead phagocytes.

Resistance The ability to withstand something, such as the effects of a drug.

Side effect An unwanted effect of a medicine.

Sulfa drug A type of medicine with antibacterial action. Sulfa drugs can cause serious side effects, including brain damage.

Tuberculosis (TB) A bacterial disease that destroys the lungs.

Turpentine A liquid made from the resin (sticky juice) of pine trees.

Index

Other Great Medical Breakthroughs

Best Avoided

Diseases are better prevented than treated. Vaccination protects people from many serious infections. When you are vaccinated, you are given a safe form of an infection as an injection or medicine. Your body's immune system figures out how to fight it, and you build up an immunity to—or defense against—the disease. If you are later exposed to the disease, this immunity can protect you. Edward Jenner developed the first vaccination in 1796. His vaccination against smallpox used pus taken from the boils of a woman with cowpox, a disease related to but less dangerous than smallpox.

Painless at Last

Surgery was much more frightening before anesthetics— medicines to prevent pain. Imagine having a tooth pulled out or an arm cut off without painkillers! Some people preferred to die. In 1846, American dentist William Morton put a man to sleep using fumes of the chemical ether and—in public —cut a tumor (a growth) from his neck. Soon everyone wanted ether for their operations.

More Blood, Please

Losing too much blood can kill you. For centuries, doctors tried transfusing (moving) blood from one person to another, but often the patient became sick and died. Then in 1901 Karl Landsteiner discovered that there are different types of blood, called blood groups. If doctors give people the suitable blood group for their body, everything is fine. With this information, blood transfusions became common, and much safer.

Top Killer Diseases

Black Death (plague), 1346–1350

Caused by a bacterium, the Black Death killed up to 250 million people in Asia and Europe. About half the people who caught it died. It can now be treated with antibiotics.

Smallpox

Caused by a virus, smallpox has killed millions of people over thousands of years. It has now been wiped out after a worldwide effort to vaccinate everyone at risk.

Influenza

Flu, caused by a virus, kills millions of people even now. From 1918 to 1920, a new strain of flu, called Spanish flu, killed up to 100 million people all around the world. Flu viruses adapt quickly, so there is no one kind of medicine that can fight all forms of flu.

Cholera

The bacterial disease cholera is passed on by drinking dirty water. It often crops up in disaster areas where there are no proper toilets or washing facilities. It can be treated with antibiotics and prevented by vaccination.

Did You Know?

- Bacteria are vital to us. Bacteria living in your gut help you digest your food and boost your immune system.

- A bacterium is a small living organism that needs to feed and reproduce.

- There are far more harmless bacteria than harmful ones. In your body, there are 10 times as many bacterial cells as human body cells!

- Sometimes people get an upset stomach after taking antibiotics. That's because the antibiotics can kill off "good" bacteria in the gut as well as the harmful bacteria that are making you sick.

- Antibiotics can't cure viral diseases. Since colds and flu are caused by viruses, there's no point in taking antibiotics if that's why you're sick.

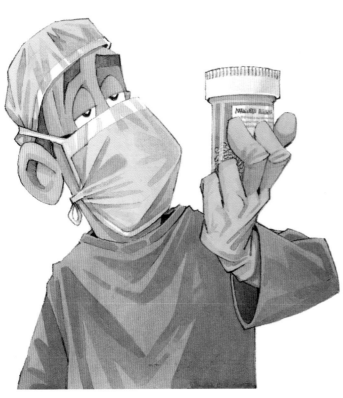

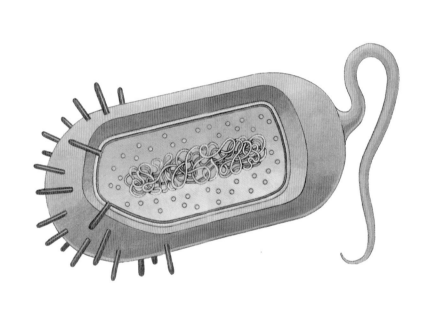